I didn't know that

crocodiles

yawn

to keep

cool

© Aladdin Books Ltd 1998
Produced by
Aladdin Books Ltd
28 Percy Street
London W1P 0LD

First published in the United States in 1998 by
Copper Beech Books,
an imprint of
The Millbrook Press
2 Old New Milford Road
Brookfield, Connecticut 06804

Concept, editorial, and design by
David West Children's Books
Designer: Robert Perry
Illustrators: James Field – Simon Girling Associates, Jo Moore

Printed in Belgium
5 4 3 2 1

Library of Congress Cataloging-in-Publication Data
Petty, Kate.
Crocodiles yawn to keep cool ; and other amazing facts about crocodiles and
alligators / by Clare Oliver ; illustrated by James Field and Jo Moore.
p. cm. — (I didn't know that—)
Includes index.
Summary: Distinguishes between crocodiles and discusses their habitats,
feeding habits, hunting behavior, reproduction, and hibernation.
ISBN 0-7613-0737-0 (hc). — ISBN 0-7613-0818-0 (lib. bdg.)
1. Crocodiles—Juvenile literature. 2. Alligators—Juvenile literature.
[1. Crocodiles. 2. Alligators.]
I. Field, James, 1959- ill. II. Moore, Jo, ill. III. Title. IV. Series.
QL666.C925O58 1998   98-6802
597.98—dc21   CIP AC

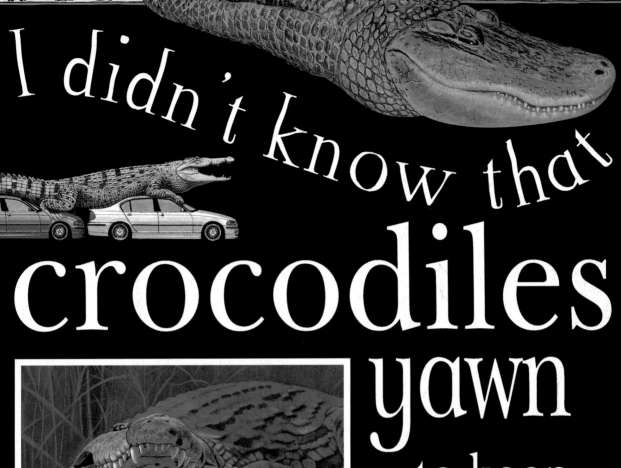

I didn't know that crocodiles yawn to keep cool

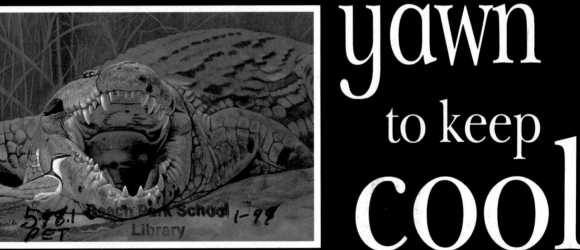

Kate Petty

COPPER BEECH BOOKS
BROOKFIELD, CONNECTICUT

I didn't know that

Introduction

Did *you* know that reptiles never stop growing? ... that some crocodiles eat people? ... that others are bred on farms, just like sheep and cows?

Discover for yourself amazing facts about crocodiles and alligators – the differences between them, where they live, what they eat, how they have babies, and more.

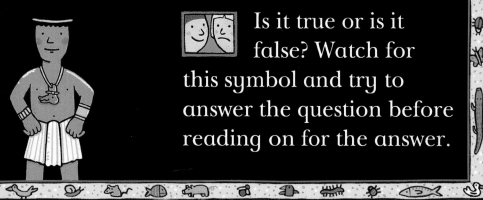

Watch for this symbol that means there is a fun project for you to try.

Is it true or is it false? Watch for this symbol and try to answer the question before reading on for the answer.

I didn't know that

crocodiles are survivors from the dinosaur age. A crocodile looked much the same in the dinosaur age as today. Crocodiles belong to a *reptile* family that wasn't wiped out 65 million years ago.

SEARCH & FIND & FIND & SEARCH

Can you find the big dinosaur?

Sarcosuchus

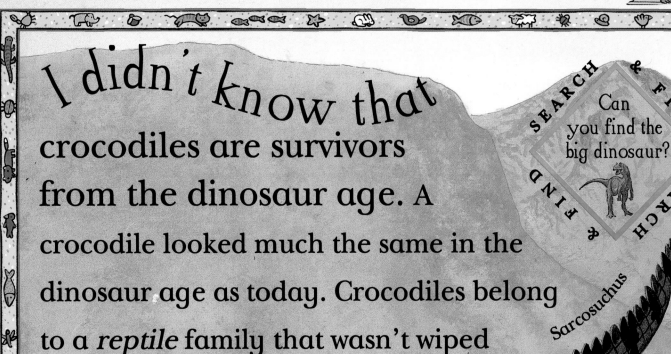

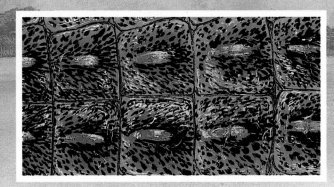

A crocodile's armor-plated skin is made up of horny scales called scutes, with extra protection from the bony plates just below the surface.

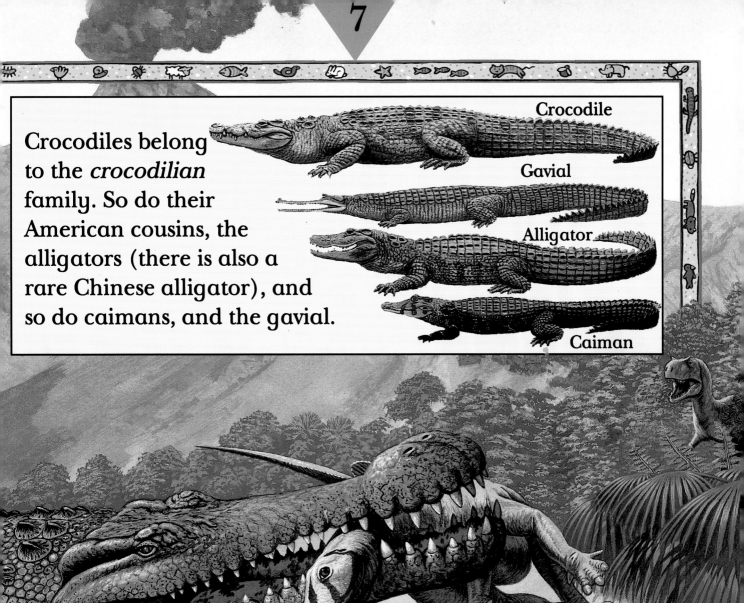

Crocodiles belong to the *crocodilian* family. So do their American cousins, the alligators (there is also a rare Chinese alligator), and so do caimans, and the gavial.

Crocodile

Gavial

Alligator

Caiman

Some *prehistoric* crocodiles were giants, some up to 40 feet long. They would almost certainly have preyed on other reptiles, including small dinosaurs.

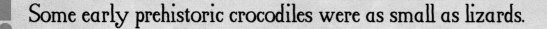

Some early prehistoric crocodiles were as small as lizards.

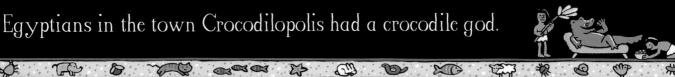

 True or false?
Crocodiles and alligators never meet.

Answer: **False**

The American crocodile is rare and the American alligator is flourishing, but both are found in the swamps of Florida.

Saltwater crocodile

Crocodiles are found in tropical areas, including Florida. Most of them live in inland waters. Crocodiles are the biggest crocodilians.

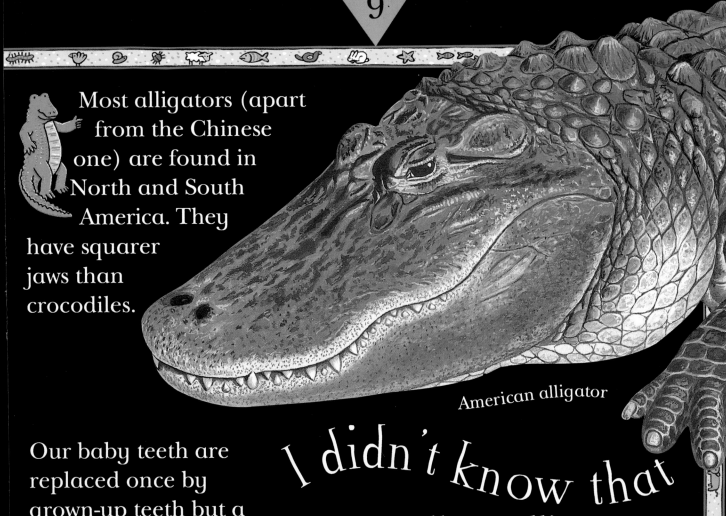

Most alligators (apart from the Chinese one) are found in North and South America. They have squarer jaws than crocodiles.

American alligator

Our baby teeth are replaced once by grown-up teeth but a crocodile's teeth can be replaced 40 times as they wear down.

I didn't know that you can tell an alligator by its teeth. Only the top teeth can be seen when the alligator's jaw is closed. A crocodile, on the other hand, shows some of its lower teeth as well.

The name "alligator" comes from "el lagarto," Spanish for "lizard."

A little bird, the Egyptian plover, is safe within the jaws of a Nile crocodile. It picks out *parasites* and leeches, doing the crocodile a favor.

Nile crocodile

I didn't know that crocodiles yawn to keep cool. Crocodiles are *cold-blooded*. They bask in the sun for warmth or cool off in the water. Cool air on the thinner skin inside their mouths stops them from overheating.

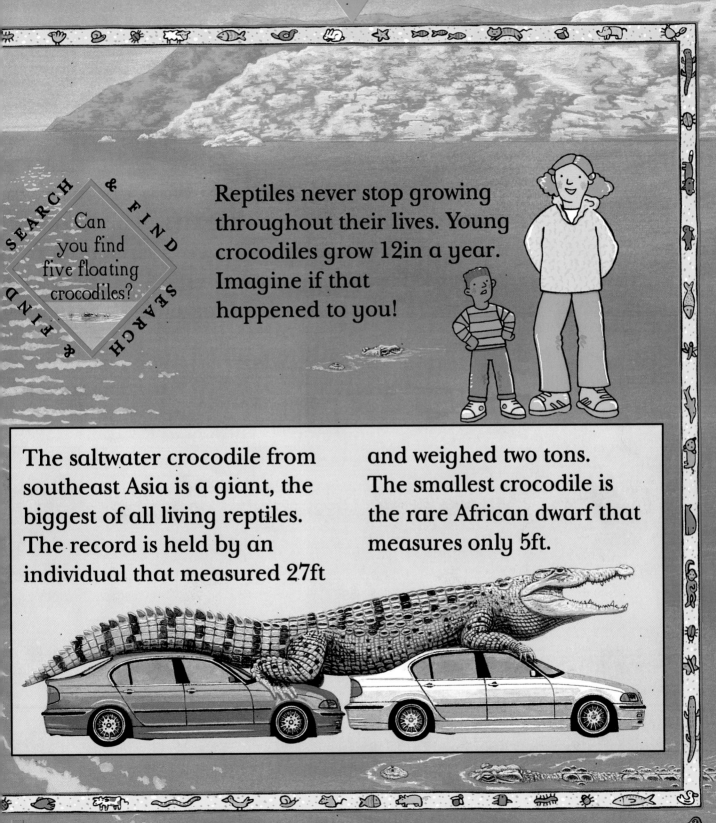

SEARCH & FIND

Can you find five floating crocodiles?

FIND SEARCH &

Reptiles never stop growing throughout their lives. Young crocodiles grow 12in a year. Imagine if that happened to you!

The saltwater crocodile from southeast Asia is a giant, the biggest of all living reptiles. The record is held by an individual that measured 27ft and weighed two tons. The smallest crocodile is the rare African dwarf that measures only 5ft.

In the movie *Peter Pan*, a crocodile swallowed a clock.

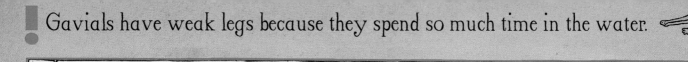

I didn't know that

crocodiles pretend to be floating logs. They lie submerged and completely still in the water. Their eyes and nostrils are on top of their heads so they can see and breathe as they lie silently in wait for their prey.

Can you find the baby caiman?

SEARCH & FIND • FIND & SEARCH

Black caiman

Some crocodiles stay underwater for an hour. Special flaps close off their nostrils, throats, and ears. A special, clear eyelid protects the eyes.

A crocodile's back feet are webbed, like a frog's. Webbed feet help it to steer and maneuver quickly in the water if it needs to.

Fish-eating crocodiles, like the Australian *freshwater* crocodile (right), often have long, thin snouts, good for catching fish, and a streamlined body.

Caimans are preyed on by anaconda snakes.

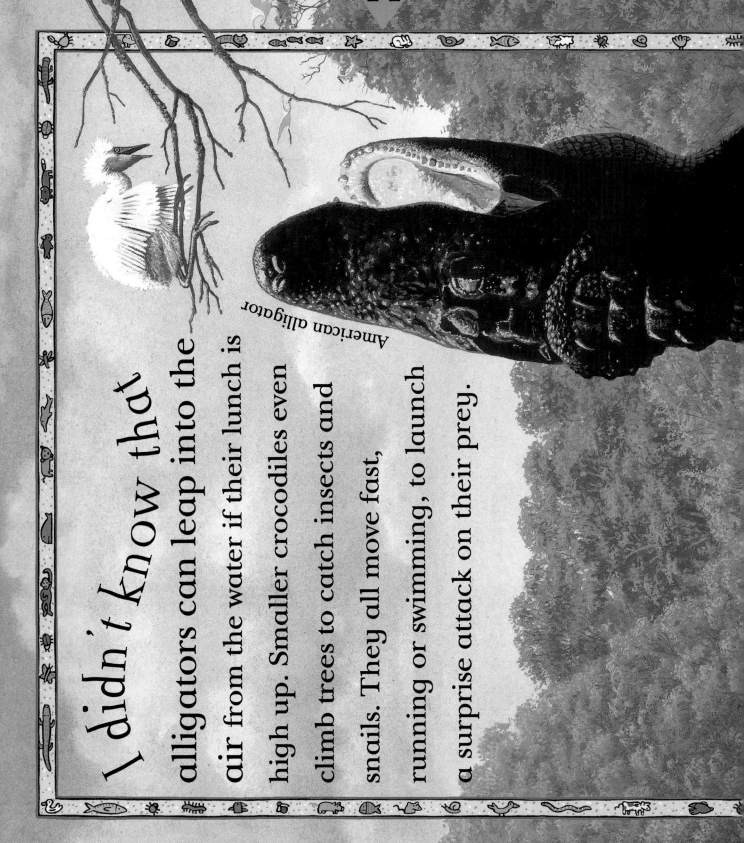

American alligator

I didn't know that

alligators can leap into the air from the water if their lunch is high up. Smaller crocodiles even climb trees to catch insects and snails. They all move fast, running or swimming, to launch a surprise attack on their prey.

The gavial catches several fish at once with a sideways swipe of its head and grips them in its sharp teeth.

True or false?

Some crocodiles are muggers.

Answer: **True**

One type of Indian crocodile is called a mugger. It is a man-eater and its main victims are women washing clothes and children playing on the riverbank.

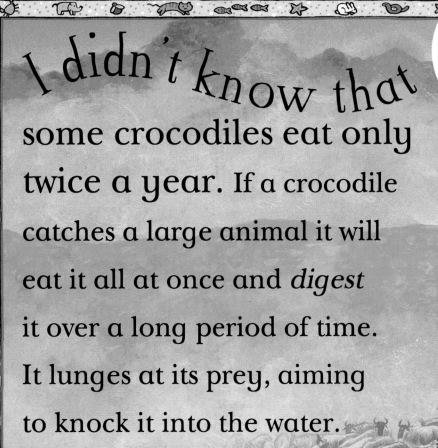

I didn't know that

some crocodiles eat only twice a year. If a crocodile catches a large animal it will eat it all at once and *digest* it over a long period of time. It lunges at its prey, aiming to knock it into the water.

Rocks have been found in the stomachs of crocodiles. They swallow them to help grind up their food.

A crocodile's teeth are designed for gripping, not for chewing. It tears the meat off in chunks and swallows them whole.

The struggle between crocodile and prey can be a tug-of-war.

Crocodiles have very strong jaws that lock on to their prey.

Nile crocodiles help each other when they feed. One holds the prey down while the other feeds off it. Groups of young Nile crocodiles cooperate to catch fish.

Wildebeest

The gavial's name comes from a word for "pot" and describes the shape of the lump on the male's nose (left). The "pot" works as an amplifier for his mating call.

Nile crocodile

In the mating season, male crocodiles behave strangely! They fight to decide who is strongest. The American crocodile (below) snaps and splashes the water with his jaws to keep others out of his *territory*.

Crocodiles can communicate using smell.

Courting couples put on *displays*, rubbing heads or lying alongside each other with their mouths open. This female saltwater crocodile raises her head out of the water to show that she wants to mate.

I didn't know that

crocodiles blow bubbles. A male Nile crocodile sometimes lowers his head into the water and blows bubbles through his nostrils. It also growls and lashes its tail as a threat to other males.

When a baby crocodile hatches it has a sharp point on its snout called an egg tooth. It needs this to break its way out of the hard-shelled egg where it has lain tightly curled.

Crocodile parents guard the nest against raiders such as birds or baboons. The parents of these eggs were caught off-guard by two thieving monitor lizards working together.

Saltwater crocodile hatchlings

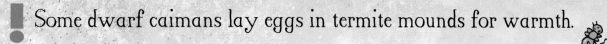
I didn't know that

crocodile eggs squeak. The *hatchlings* let their mother know when they are ready to come out. High-pitched noises from inside the shells bring the mother to scrape off the nest coverings that kept them warm.

A mother crocodile makes a nest on land where her eggs can be kept safe and warm. She makes it in the same place every year. She lays the eggs at night, a few at a time, and covers them.

21

The teeth of baby crocodiles are as sharp as needles.

SEARCH & FIND Can you find the kingfisher? FIND & SEARCH

I didn't know that crocodiles carry their babies in pouches. A mother crocodile has a pouch in the bottom of her mouth. As soon as the babies hatch she picks them up one by one and carefully takes them to the water.

Mother and father watch over the young crocodiles in a "nursery" at the waterside. The babies catch their own small fish and crabs while the parents keep watch.

Mugger crocodile

Crocodile and alligator babies cannot look after themselves very well. A young alligator may hitch a ride on its mother's back.

I didn't know that

some crocodiles swim in the sea. The estuarine – or saltwater – crocodile from Southeast Asia and Australia is the biggest of all crocodiles and the only one to swim in the sea. It lives in *estuaries* along the coast.

SEARCH & FIND
Can you find five turtles?
FIND & SEARCH

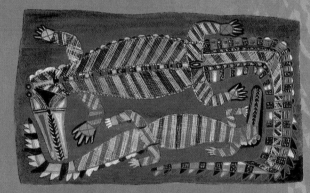

Australian aboriginal art often contains pictures of crocodiles. This is because according to their ancient beliefs the spirits of the dead live on in crocodiles.

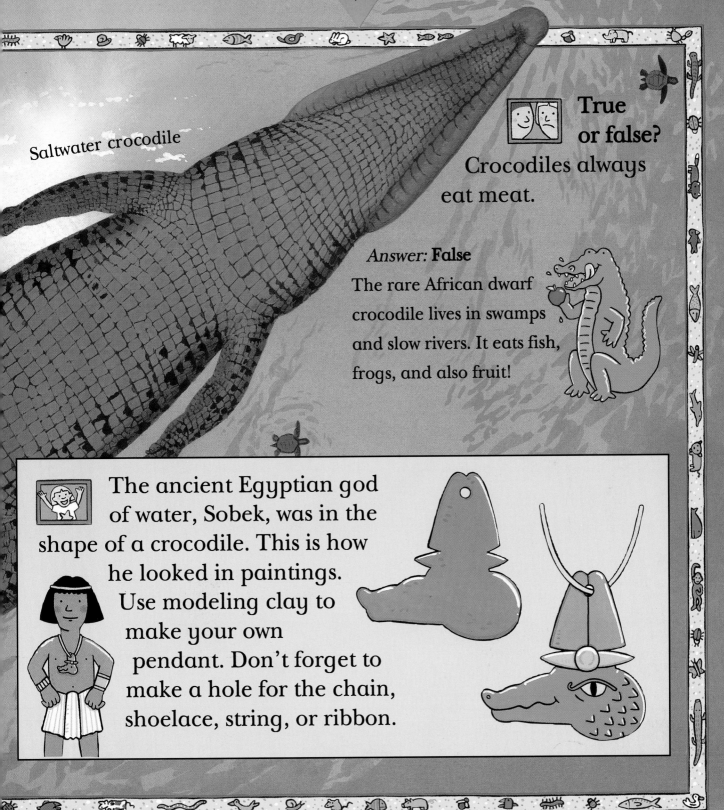

Saltwater crocodile

True or false?

Crocodiles always eat meat.

Answer: **False**
The rare African dwarf crocodile lives in swamps and slow rivers. It eats fish, frogs, and also fruit!

The ancient Egyptian god of water, Sobek, was in the shape of a crocodile. This is how he looked in paintings. Use modeling clay to make your own pendant. Don't forget to make a hole for the chain, shoelace, string, or ribbon.

The so-called "false" gavial is in fact a crocodile.

I didn't know that

some alligators sleep through winter.
Alligators dig holes and passages underground
where they can escape the heat and
cold. Chinese alligators and the most
northerly American alligators
hibernate in these tunnels.

SEARCH & FIND & FIND SEARCH & SEARCH & FIND
Can you find the snake?

There are only 600 of these Chinese alligators left living in the wild. They are protected by law but *poachers* still kill them for their skins and meat.

The dwarf caiman from the Amazon basin is one of the smallest alligators. Caimans live in South America. They have armor on their backs and their bellies.

There have been reports of alligators using sewers as their tunnels.

In 1972, crocodile hunting was banned in Australia. It is believed that around 270,000 saltwater crocodile skins and between 200,000 and 300,000 freshwater crocodile skins were exported from Australia before the ban.

Scientists can learn about crocodiles by fitting them with radio transmitters. That way they can keep track of the crocodiles' movements and find out where they go.

28

I didn't know that

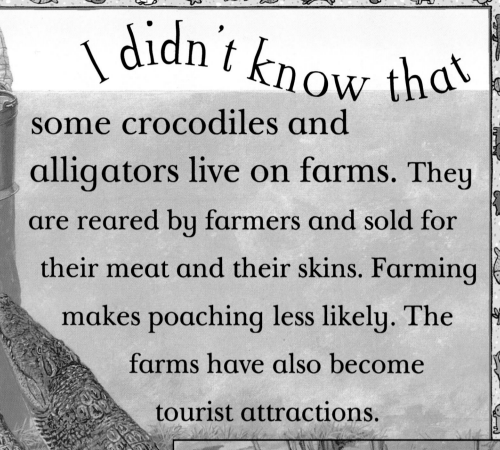

some crocodiles and alligators live on farms. They are reared by farmers and sold for their meat and their skins. Farming makes poaching less likely. The farms have also become tourist attractions.

Some people like to keep baby broad-nosed caimans as pets. They look cute when they are very small, but are less fun when they grow bigger!

Glossary

Cold-blooded
Animals that take their heat from the temperature outside are cold-blooded.

Crocodilian
The ancient reptile family that includes crocodiles, alligators, caimans, and gavials.

Digest
What an animal's body does with food before taking the nutrients into the bloodstream.

Display
The way in which animals show off to each other, for example, when a peacock spreads its tail feathers.

Estuary
The place where a river runs into the sea.

Fossils
Remains of plants and animals in the rocks. These remains can be dated to show how many millions of years ago a particular plant or animal lived.

Freshwater
Freshwater creatures are

found inland in rivers, streams, and lakes – not in the salt water of the sea.

Hatchling
An animal that has just come out of its egg.

Hibernate
To sleep through the winter months.

Parasite
A creature that lives off other creatures, for example a flea.

Poachers
People who hunt and trap animals that are protected by the law.

Prehistoric
The time before there were any written records.

Reptile
The animal family to which snakes, crocodiles, and dinosaurs all belong.

Territory
An area where an animal lives, which it will defend against outsiders.

Index